The Certain Body

Also by Julia Guez

In an Invisible Glass Case Which Is Also a Frame

Equestrian Monuments by Luis Chaves
(co-translated with Samantha Zighelboim)

The Certain Body

Julia Guez

Four Way Books
Tribeca

For
Meredith Lash
Jan Niemira
&
Winnie Varghese

LIBRARY OF CONGRESS CATALOGING-IN-PUBLICATION DATA

Names: Guez, Julia, author.
Title: The certain body / Julia Guez.
Description: New York : Four Way Books, [2022]
Identifiers: LCCN 2022003879 | ISBN 9781954245303 (paperback) | ISBN 9781954245389 (epub)
Subjects: LCGFT: Poetry.
Classification: LCC PS3607.U4716 C47 2022 | DDC 811/.6--dc23/eng/20220128
LC record available at https://lccn.loc.gov/2022003879

Four Way Books is a not-for-profit literary press. We are grateful for the assistance we receive from individual donors, public arts agencies, and private foundations including the NEA, NEA Cares, Literary Arts Emergency Fund, and the New York State Council on the Arts, a state agency.

We are a proud member of the Community of Literary Magazines and Presses.

Contents

One

Two

Three

Notes

Assured of certain certainties,

—T.S. Eliot, "Preludes"

One

MEDITATION AT CALLICOON

More and more night pretends
it isn't spring. What to
make of the daffodils then?
Hyacinth here and there, wind
and rain? So many birds.
Of course they won't stay
long. None of this will.
Not the night, the cold,
the city full of swallows.
Not the bridges and rivers.
Not the sea, no god
born of the sea foam.
Not even mothers and sons
this would be unbearable without.

Still Life with Insufficient iCloud Storage

And here we are—   sewing
secrets we have wanted in some form

to keep,   sewing
them into the sky, sewing them into

the lining of a lake   in the sky
as if there's no violence

the cloud cannot hold   there, where
rain comes from

remembering to fall   again and again
saying, Hoi Polloi,

I am one of you.   Susceptible to
rust and moths,

I may even be   taken
in the night by thieves.

Like so many   seeds and spores, lost
in the small hands of the wind.

THE CERTAIN BODY

after Vija Celmins

Each taking months to
sand, surfaces made aware
of their own precarity
and also the miracle
of them being here
in this museum, given
all the forces arrayed
against seeing the same
night so long, same
sky, same city of
stars (not the same
at all) repeating themselves
on this body of
water whose waves italicize
across a canvas meant
to remember the real
thing, painted stones whose
stoniness fix the image
in memory—

As We Consider Another Child

What hasn't been taken from us

by now (or it too would've gone

the way of the flatware)

must be genetic.

The difference between

inheritance and inheritance:

curtains, pearls, words once

half-dressed in concern

Presbyterian to the point

of incomprehensible after noon.

What you can quit

and what, of course, you can't

passes from one

century to the next.

Fair to fear

what's lying in wait

in these cells, if or when

it will wax red and rise

bone-white,

dragonish, drawling. Fore-

knowing the trauma, entering on it

with full consent of the will and why,

if she's nothing but a madrigal and then some,

should we not hope for dahlias?

The rent is due at the end of each month.

At the end of each month

the same question then,

sleeplessness—and yes,

novenas, TV, nausea.

IF INDEED I AM ILL,

Tell me all about London, the weather there
in spring outside the walls of the Great Hall.

These things matter less to me than the sound
of your summary, shadows cast on the watery

surfaces of my mind by invisible fingers
whose energy is everything, as you know.

These sonatas, these scores, tell me
what of them will last when everything falls away—

Still Life with SARS-CoV-2

and then what
and then
what, what
then

In a New Form

She's not taking her temperature first thing in the morning, not the
   way she was before.

   The slow passing of a cortège in March sleet, the poverty.

The thermometer is on my windowsill now.

   Nothing seems real or right.

She doesn't even ask if it would be safe to borrow.

   Now it is April and another summer.

What is written in small red letters,
above the display:

   Days may be where we live, but mornings are eternity.
   They wake us, and every day waking is absurdity;
   All the things you just did yesterday to do over again, eternally.

It used to sit on the convex
frame of a mirror hanging
on her side of this
bed we haven't shared in weeks.

There is saying the same thing again in a different form,
There is saying something new in the same form,
There is saying the same thing again in the same form,
There is not much saying something new in a new form.

Isolation, etcetera—
quarantine
within
quarantine—
timor mortis conturbat me.

      Coughing in fog

beside a wrinkled bed, I clean the thing repeatedly with a lemon-
    scented wipe.

      What will survive of us?
      Larkin thought the answer might be "love,"
      But couldn't prove it.

Not sure how the battery isn't low
by now. (I am so low
now.) We have been

brought to our knees by this
terror very close
to pure terror
prolonging itself so

> that there is no necessary season for things
> and birth and death happen on adjacent wards,
> that both are labour, halting and starting;
> that women are always the middlemen
> finding the coins . . .

a sensor at the very end, spelling the word,

> Spring. Spring.

> *If you do not weep now, you may never weep.*

> This is the world and the entropy of things.

> This is the city's archipelago, its dead—

> Now nothing will ever be the same again.
> And everything will be as it always was.

Two

A More Onerous Citizenship

I.

Wednesday

So many Cassandras sing each to each. What we, gathering, cannot
    yet sense

may as well be Greek.

For the record, I do not know Greek.

Let there be a record.

Let the record show my Greeklessness would matter greatly at
    several points,

one or two in particular.

May have been windwarding. The song, I mean.

All those xylophones.

Windwarding now to know the music was both knowable and known then, when

I was standing next to you in the last pew (with our coats still on

because it was cold

and we would still have been hurrying to certain offices

after). I will think of you often.

Performing these frail rites to bend the centrifugal back some,

I am afraid

this will be one convalescence after another,

lilacs on every sill

profusely sad knowing they too spread and spread.

Not unlike the bells,

ever-widening rings of all kinds and the terrible swing of the censer, sirens on the other side of this psalm

whose linens are loud with cries, and are become our Italies.

II.

Thursday

I was made American. You must consider this

wanting, badly, to be washed

clean in that light.

Consider also the fever-dream:

in my case, fractals

which may or may not belong

to otters who appear to be holding

hands. I see the pair, so much dun-

colored fur folding in on itself—

I see the dark river.

Fortunately, there is also

a shower scene. I thank God for this

part of the dream,

the smell of that

soap and all

the seminarians there

with me and my wife.

In the dim light of this painterly *onsen*

glistening

bodies, one is pale

but not at all sickly—

pearlescent then—yes and lissome,

lithe.

Breasts not unlike a murmuration of birds.

What they fever after, we fever after

in tight swaths, circling

the warmest water

laving

feet, fascia, calves,

the small of so many backs,

homily of so many hands

lathering once bleeding *eidolons*—

every single scar

a story whose ending is clearly not one

for here we are

gently washing, washed

III.

Friday

How to mourn
how many the
stations of the
breath have taken.
After the first
death, there is
no other, but
the requiem is
endless, endless the
sequelae whose ever-
widening rings widen
around the names
of the dead
swallowing those who
survive them. Exactly
why we survive
and can look
back with furrowed
brow is beyond
me. It is

not something to
know. On this
day ministers enter
in silence—no
one there—the
force of that
and also the
very fact that
they go on
with this ritual
calling for some
relief from beyond
the desolating sound
of songbirds going
on and on
in the cemetery
the same way
they do here.

IV.

Saturday

Between that disgust and this

one, a vigil;

the dark has never been final.

V.

Sunday

Apparently Arab scholars, when
speaking of the text,
use this admirable expression:

the certain body.
What body?
We have several of them.

This one is not sleeping.
Night is a time of quiet then:
a time to sort, to make bargains,

promises and plans
even if they're all provisional.
Night is a time to weep

without the children there to see
and when the weeping is over,
night is a time to read and write.

If we write, we are in debt.
If we write, we owe.
This debt transverses all writing;

it shapes it. It gives it life.
This debt is connected to bodies
at work: gendered bodies, material

bodies, bodies in conflict.
We have several of them
the city is not sure what to do with.

Poor coroners, the poor
morgue, so many unmourned
they pile up

in trucks by the road
to the contagious hospital.
The body of anatomists and physiologists,

the one science sees or discusses:
this is the text of grammarians,
critics, commentators.

The cells of this text,
a complex system of letters,
combine

moon blood and wings
with
the motility of horses—

too many to count—
cantering
into this pact forming,

as you well know, a word
built to withstand
many things.

(All but one, in fact.)
We also have a body of bliss
consisting solely of erotic

relations, utterly distinct
from the first body:
it is another contour,

another nomination;
thus with the text and the flesh
of a real intertext:

the mouth's wet
vestibule, warm and red baring
brass and wind,

Glenlivet and cunnilingus
whispering
the same words across time

into the same ear
bringing itself so close
droplets land on the same lobe

before waves of sound
hurry towards the tympanum,
through doors of three

ossicles and at least one
cochlea,
leewarding to find

the soft parts, feeling
inside the word
we have been whispering to each other

for centuries about
sleeplessness, Brahms, starlings,
greed and ghosts

who would have wept to step
barefoot into reality and cried
out to feel it again

the way we do now.
The sun rises
over so much we have been

whispering about for millennia—
war, weather,
medicine and how, finally, to explain

the day. For all we have done
to extinguish this
democracy, here it is:

the brightest eye blinking across the sky,
a kindness the color of orioles,
bread and cellos meant for everyone.

THREE

Still Life When All Our Symptoms Seem to Have Symptoms of Their Own

the dark is very dark

on the night-side of things,
long is very long.

My heart is feathered

fire, smallest
flying flag,

wings are sad,

sad, singing
not at all slow.

My heart

closes
in on itself not

unlike a peony

whose own process of
becoming has been

set back until

the open-handed
flower is tight and green

like a fist, poor thing is

thrumming in this
invisible glass case

which is also a frame

where the most
contagious are taken

to be alone

there all together,
praying the same prayer—

Ode

The leech and the lachrymal are a no go now. We must devise our
    own cures.

By the pew,
        a booth. Do not stop there. There may very well be another

garden beyond the garden in the courtyard. And at some point, high
    walls.

Do not let them deter you, though—
        they are only ornamental.

In one of these gardens, you will find a set of keys

by the arbor
        not far from a pond filled with coins.

You will think to yourself, This is it. (It isn't.)

I will be waiting
        on the very next lawn

with a hand of bananas on a blanket, some SmartWater, sandwiches
    and a sign

there to say,

you are closer than you think.

Still Life with Post-Acute Sequelae of SARS-CoV-2

and then what
and then
what, what
then

VENI CORONABERIS

Come, come and be crowned.

On the Occasion of My Half-Birthday

Thyme out in the window box,
      wildness and splay of what has always survived winter here,
      fasting only to re-emerge greener in the spring.

All I want is the sun on my face.
      At the park where I take our children to play,
      I want my whole body to feel

light pouring through the leaves
      on massive branches with a force that can finally be
      honest about its own ambition

to draw the citrus and myrrh
      out of this or any other afternoon, knowing weeks of them,
      knowing months and years disappear

like so many Simeons—

Hymn, Then

after Jammie Holmes

It is the please, George.
As in, asking these in-
tolerable things to be
other than what
they have always been
and but politely.
Inside the throat,
a hymn then
one May when
the sun refused
to shine on
the final please
hanging above the city
for all to see
the certain body
gathering force in-
struments of war,
weather—heat now
rain—hate, even
a plague cannot contain.

Forty

All the purple flowers,
the way they fall,
white and purple, falling.
See how they turn
their skirts, turning their
white and purple skirts,
so that at least
they fall slowly, make
no sound, beginning soon
to yellow then brown.

Notes

The Certain Body

And art exists that one may recover the sensation of life; it exists to make one feel things, to make the stone *stony*. The purpose of art is to impart the sensation of things as they are perceived and not as they are known.

Viktor Shklovsky, "Art as Technique"

The Vija Celmins retrospective at The MET Breuer (September 24, 2019 through January 12, 2020) was titled "To Fix the Image in Memory."

As We Consider Another Child

the poetry of the future has got to have a lot of nerve. it's got to come from at least three brains: the brain in the head, the gut-brain, and the brain in the ovaries. it will wax red and rise bone-white. the poetry of the future will be nutritious and opulent.

Maggie Nelson, "the future of poetry," *The Latest Winter*

To be older and grateful

That this time you too were half-grateful
The pangs had begun—prepared
And clear-headed, foreknowing

The trauma, entering on it
With full consent of the will.

Seamus Heaney, "A Pillowed Head," *Opened Ground: Selected Poems, 1966-1996*

If Indeed I Am Ill,

"If Indeed I Am Ill," is for Kamilah Aisha Moon.

In a New Form

Every indentation signals a line or lines from "You, Very Young in New York," "Repeat Until Time," or "The Sandpit After Rain."

Hannah Sullivan, *Three Poems*

A More Onerous Citizenship

Illness is the night-side of life, a more onerous citizenship.

Susan Sontag, *Illness as Metaphor*

I.

I have heard the mermaids singing, each to each.

I do not think they will sing to me.

T.S. Eliot, "The Love Song of J. Alfred Prufrock," *Selected Poems*

Miserere mei, Deus (Psalm 51) begins: "Have mercy on me, O God."

"Ash Wednesday," *The Book of Common Prayer*

The bended lanes are loud with cries,
And are become our Italies,

Thomas Merton, "The City's Spring," *The Collected Poems of Thomas Merton*

II.

I was made American. You must consider this.

Lucie Brock-Broido, "Dove, Interrupted," *Stay, Illusion*

Twice and twice
(Again the smoking souvenir,
Bleeding eidolon!) and yet again.
Until the bright logic is won . . .

Hart Crane, "Legend," *White Buildings*

III.

I shall not murder
The mankind of her going with a grave truth
Nor blaspheme down the stations of the breath
With any further
Elegy of innocence and youth.

Deep with the first dead lies London's daughter,
Robed in the long friends,
The grains beyond age, the dark veins of her mother,
Secret by the unmourning water
Of the riding Thames.
After the first death, there is no other.

Dylan Thomas, "A Refusal to Mourn the Death, by Fire, of a Child in London," *The Poems of Dylan Thomas*

Exactly why we survive and can look back with furrowed brow is beyond me.

It is not something to know.

Claudia Rankine, *CITIZEN*

On this day the ministers enter in silence.

"Good Friday," *The Book of Common Prayer*

IV.

Between that disgust and this, between the things
That are on the dump (azaleas and so on)
And those that will be (azaleas and so on),
One feels the purifying change.

Wallace Stevens, "The Man on the Dump," *Parts of a World*

V.

Apparently Arab scholars, when speaking of the text, use this admirable
expression: *the certain body.* What body? We have several of them; the
body of anatomists and physiologists, the one science sees or discusses:
this is the text of grammarians, critics, commentators, philologists (the
pheno-text). But we also have a body of bliss consisting solely of erotic
relations, utterly distinct from the first body: it is another contour,
another nomination; thus with the text.

Roland Barthes, *The Pleasure of the Text* (Translated by Richard Miller)

If we write, we are in debt. If we write, we owe. This debt transverses all
writing; it shapes it. It gives it life. Legitimacy. This debt is connected to
bodies at work: gendered bodies, material bodies, bodies in conflict.

Cristina Rivera Garza, "The Unusual: A Manifesto," *Pen Transmissions*

By the road to the contagious hospital

William Carlos Williams, [By the road to the contagious hospital],
Spring and All

They were those that would have wept to step barefoot into reality,
That would have wept and been happy, have shivered in the frost
And cried out to feel it again . . .

Wallace Stevens, "Large Red Man Reading," *The Auroras of Autumn*

Still Life When All Our Symptoms Seem to Have Symptoms of Their Own

feathered
fire,
smallest
flying
flag,
petal of silenced peoples,
syllable
of buried blood . . .

Pablo Neruda, "Ode to a Hummingbird," *Selected Odes* (Translated by Margaret Sayers Peden)

Ode

"Ode" is for Grace Guez.

Veni Coronaberis

Who never lost, are unprepared
A Coronet to find!
Who never thirsted
Flagons, and Cooling Tamarind!

Emily Dickinson, No. 73, *The Complete Poems of Emily Dickinson*

On the Occasion of My Half-Birthday

Found in Luke 2:29–32, [the Song of Simeon] is called the *Nunc Dimittis* for its first words in the Vulgate Bible: *Nunc dimittis servum tuum, Domine, secundum verbum tuum, in pace* ("Now, Master, you can let your servant go in peace, just as you promised"). Because of its implications of fulfillment, peace, and rest, the early church viewed it as appropriate for the ending of the day. Since the 4th century it has been used in such evening worship services as Compline, Vespers, and Evensong.

"Nunc Dimittis," *Encyclopaedia Britannica*

Hymn, Then

"Hymn, Then" is for George Floyd.

Were you there when the sun refused to shine? (Were you there?)
Were you there when the sun refused to shine?
O sometimes it causes me to tremble! tremble! tremble!
Were you there when the sun refused to shine?

The Hymnal 1982, #172

Acknowledgments

Many thanks to the following magazines and anthologies where some of this work has previously appeared (sometimes in a slightly different form): *128 Lit*: "A More Onerous Citizenship"; *Adroit*: "The Certain Body"; *The Literary Review*: "Still Life with Insufficient iCloud Storage"; *Blunderbuss*: "As We Consider Another Child"; *Together in a Sudden Strangeness: American Poets Respond to the Pandemic* (Knopf, 2020): "If Indeed I Am Ill,"; *Ocean State Review*: "In a New Form" and "Ode"; *A Fire to Light Our Tongues* (Texas Christian University, 2022): "Still Life When All Our Symptoms Seem to Have Symptoms of Their Own"; *The Cortland Review*: "On the Occasion of My Half-Birthday"; *The Scores*: "Hymn, Then"; *Queer Poem-A-Day*: "Forty."

Many thanks to the following writers, editors, artists and friends for insight and encouragement throughout the process of building *The Certain Body*: Jason Boulanger, Rule Brand, Emily Brandt, Romy Cossack, Andrew Dansby, Elizabeth Dell, Jay Deshpande, Timothy Donnelly, Joshua and Nalini Edwin, Patrick Errington, Andrew Felsher, Elisa Gonzalez, Devin Gael Kelly, Christian Gullette, Lisa Hiton, Regan Jacks, Peter LaBerge, Brett Fletcher Lauer, Beth Harrison, Gary Hawkins, John James, Charles Kell, Jason Koo, Saad Mahmoud, Justin Maki, Ricardo Maldonado, Paco Márquez, Craig Morgan Teicher, Michael Morse, Jerome Murphy, Veer Nannavatty, Michael O'Connor, Minna Proctor, Ruben Quesada, Alice Quinn, David Roderick, Sam Ross, Allison Serafin, Gerald and Kacy Shepps, Emily Sernaker, Julia Shipley, Fritha Strand, Benjamin Stroman, Leah Umanksy, Donna Walker-Nixon, Samantha Zighelboim and Rachel Zucker.

For the art, many thanks to Julie Mehretu. For the photograph, many thanks to Wesley Mann. For perspective on what this work means to be at its very best, many thanks to Kazim Ali, t'ai freedom ford, sam sax and Jenny Xie.

Many thanks to everyone at Four Way Books, especially Sally Ball, Clarissa Long, Hannah Matheson, Ryan Murphy and Martha Rhodes. Thanks, also, to Frederick Courtright for securing all of the permissions for these notes. Thanks, finally, to Jonathan Blunk, for copyediting *The Certain Body* with such care.

Many thanks to all of my colleagues at Teach For America New York, especially Jennifer Early-Quinchia, Charissa Fernandez, Priscilla Forsyth, Myra Gupta, Aarti Marajh, Tia Morris and Margaux Zanelli-Lampariello.

At Rutgers University Writers House, many thanks to Aimee Labrie. At NYU, many thanks to Joanna Yas and Deborah Landau.

Many thanks to my teachers and to my students.

Many thanks to Dr. Meredith Lash-Dardia, Jan Niemira and Reverend Winnie Varghese for seeing me through the first seventy-five days. Thanks, also, to Dr. Ally Halbig and Dr. Thea McCallion for seeing me through the weeks and months since.

Thanks, most of all, to my big-hearted wife and sons.

Julia Guez is a writer and translator based in the city of New York. Her essays, interviews, fiction, poetry and translations have appeared in *Guernica, POETRY, The Guardian, BOMB, The Brooklyn Rail*, and *Kenyon Review*. She has been awarded the Discovery/*Boston Review* Poetry Prize, a Fulbright Fellowship and The John Frederick Nims Memorial Prize in Translation as well as a translation fellowship from the National Endowment for the Arts. For the last decade, Guez has worked with Teach For America New York; she's currently the senior managing director of design and implementation. She teaches creative writing at NYU and Rutgers. You can find more of her work online at www.juliaguez.net

Publication of this book was made possible by grants and donations. We are also grateful to those individuals who participated in our 2021 Build a Book Program. They are:

Anonymous (16), Maggie Anderson, Susan Kay Anderson, Kristina Andersson, Kate Angus, Kathy Aponick, Sarah Audsley, Jean Ball, Sally Ball, Clayre Benzadón, Greg Blaine, Laurel Blossom, adam bohannon, Betsy Bonner, Lee Briccetti, Joan Bright, Jane Martha Brox, Susan Buttenwieser, Anthony Cappo, Carla and Steven Carlson, Paul and Brandy Carlson, Renee Carlson, Alice Christian, Karen Rhodes Clarke, Mari Coates, Jane Cooper, Ellen Cosgrove, Peter Coyote, Robin Davidson, Kwame Dawes, Michael Anna de Armas, Brian Komei Dempster, Renko and Stuart Dempster, Matthew DeNichilo, Rosalynde Vas Dias, Kent Dixon, Patrick Donnelly, Lynn Emanuel, Blas Falconer, Elliot Figman, Jennifer Franklin, Helen Fremont and Donna Thagard, Gabriel Fried, John Gallaher, Reginald Gibbons, Jason Gifford, Jean and Jay Glassman, Dorothy Tapper Goldman, Sarah Gorham and Jeffrey Skinner, Lauri Grossman, Julia Guez, Sarah Gund, Naomi Guttman and Jonathan Mead, Kimiko Hahn, Mary Stewart Hammond, Beth Harrison, Jeffrey Harrison, Melanie S. Hatter, Tom Healy and Fred Hochberg, K.T. Herr, Karen Hildebrand, Joel Hinman, Deming Holleran, Lillian Howan, Thomas and Autumn Howard, Catherine Hoyser, Elizabeth Jackson, Jessica Jacobs and Nickole Brown, Christopher Johanson, Jen Just, Maeve Kinkead, Alexandra Knox, Lindsay and John Landes, Suzanne Langlois, Laura Lauth, Sydney Lea, David Lee and Jamila Trindle, Rodney Terich Leonard, Jen Levitt, Howard Levy, Owen Lewis, Matthew Lippman, Jennifer Litt, Karen Llagas, Sara London and Dean Albarelli, Clarissa Long, James Longenbach, Cynthia Lowen, Ralph and Mary Ann Lowen, Ricardo Maldonado, Myra Malkin, Jacquelyn Malone, Carrie Mar, Kathleen McCoy, Ellen McCulloch-Lovell, Lupe Mendez, David Miller, Josephine Miller, Nicki Moore, Guna Mundheim, Matthew Murphy and Maura Rockcastle, Michael and Nancy Murphy, Myra Natter, Jay Baron Nicorvo, Ashley Nissler, Kimberly Nunes, Rebecca and Daniel Okrent, Robert Oldshue and Nina Calabresi, Kathleen Ossip, Judith Pacht, Cathy McArthur Palermo, Marcia and Chris Pelletiere, Sam Perkins, Susan Peters and Morgan Driscoll, Patrick Phillips,

Robert Pinsky, Megan Pinto, Connie Post, Kyle Potvin, Grace Prasad, Kevin Prufer, Alicia Jo Rabins, Anna Duke Reach, Victoria Redel, Martha Rhodes, Paula Rhodes, Louise Riemer, Sarah Santner, Amy Schiffman, Peter and Jill Schireson, Roni and Richard Schotter, James and Nancy Shalek, Soraya Shalforoosh, Peggy Shinner, Anita Soos, Donna Spruijt-Metz, Ann F. Stanford, Arlene Stang, Page Hill Starzinger, Marina Stuart, Yerra Sugarman, Marjorie and Lew Tesser, Eleanor Thomas, Tom Thompson and Miranda Field, James Tjoa, Ellen Bryant Voigt, Connie Voisine, Moira Walsh, Ellen Dore Watson, Calvin Wei, John Wender, Eleanor Wilner, Mary Wolf, and Pamela and Kelly Yenser.